True Stories

of the

Erie Canal

Compiled and Edited

By Donna Winters

Copyright © 2012 Donna Winters

All Rights Reserved.

Published by
Bigwater Publishing
PO Box 85
Garden, MI 49835
www.GreatLakesRomances.com

ISBN: 0-934048-53-7
ISBN-13: 978-0923048-53-2

Contents of this volume have been excerpted and adapted from:

Rochester and its Early Canal Days

By Capt. H.P. Marsh (1914)

Five Years on the Erie Canal: An Account of Some of the Most Striking Scenes and Incidents, During Five Years' Labor on the Erie Canal

By M. Eaton (1845)

The Girl Who Ran Away

Excerpted from *Rochester and its Early Canal Days* by Capt. H.P. Marsh (1914).

I arrived in the city in the afternoon, and just at dark sauntered up to Exchange Street Bridge. At that time it was a common high bridge, before hoist or swing bridges had been invented.

I was standing on the bridge, watching the boats gliding underneath, when a man with rather unsteady steps came up to me and said, "Do you know where I can get a steersman?"

"I can steer a boat. I'm out of a berth and will engage with you for $30 per month, including board.

"All right." He shook my hand. "My other steersman will meet us at Pittsford tomorrow, where we will load with potatoes for New York City. We usually carry flour, as my boat is a Rochester Line boat, but there is no load ready at present. Go aboard and tell the cook to dish you up something, if you are hungry; there's the craft in the slip." He motioned toward a nicely painted ball head boat lying in the old packet basin.

The captain stumbled along toward Wheeler's grocery and day boat barn. Wheeler's, like all canal groceries, kept a bar. It was on the towpath side, and the building can still be seen just above the Exchange Street Bridge.

I went aboard, knocked at the cabin hatch before going down, and being hungry, told the girl what the captain said.

She did not speak at first, but looked frightened, and placed some cold meat, potatoes, and bread and butter before me, and said she would warm up the potatoes and make tea, but as there appeared to be no fire, I told her not to do it, as that was plenty good enough.

She looked as though she had been weeping and seemed afraid.

I made my way to the hands' cabin, in the forward part of the boat. Having matches, I struck a light, found the lamp, stirred up an old bunk, and turned in for a good sleep. I did not go to sleep, however, but thought of the sad-looking girl in the captain's cabin. I concluded it was his daughter and he had scolded her, or she expected him back drunk, or both, as that is what I thought his condition would be as he staggered towards Wheeler's grocery.

I must have fallen asleep, but the captain coming aboard awakened me. Then there were voices apparently in argument, the captain swearing, and knowing he could be swearing at no one but the girl, I opened the door leading from the hands' cabin into the midship. Hearing scuffling, I dropped down from where I was and walked back under deck to the cabin aft. There, I learned that the girl was not the captain's daughter. Then she screamed, and I heard the captain chasing her with unsteady footsteps.

The door leading from his cabin into the midship was not fastened, so I pushed it open, and as he came to that side, I reached into the cabin, grabbed the skipper by the legs, and jerked him through the door. He fell heavily on the keelson, which is a heavy piece of wood running through the middle of the boat from stem to stern. It was about breast high from the midship to the cabin floor, and thus stunned him when striking.

I did not stop to see whether he was alive or not, but climbed up through the hole where I had pulled the captain, shut and bolted the door, and turned to the trembling girl.

"You are all right, now, don't be afraid. If he isn't dead now, I'll kill him anyway. Pack up your things if you have any, and I will go with you to the police station, and you can tell your story to them."

Then she cried and said she did not want to go anywhere but home.

I then heard the captain swearing and stumbling around inside, so I ran up on deck, forward to my cabin, ran down, shut and bolted the door leading from there to the midship, where the captain was. Then I knew we were safe, for without outside help, or tools, he could never get out.

I ran back, got the girl and her small bundle ashore, then yelled to the captain, who was mumbling curses, to shut up, or I would go down and brain him! I could be brave on the outside with the Cap a prisoner, and I had an old single barrelled pistol and one load, about as dangerous as a mosquito's bite.

The girl said she lived about six miles up the river, and that she could walk, for she had seen all she wanted of Rochester. Her home was near to what is now called the Junction, and is on the Pennsylvania Railroad where it crosses the West Shore, in one of the houses on the river road from Plymouth Avenue in the city, through the little village called the Rapids at that time.

No one had heard the rumpus, as that was the only boat in the slip that night and policemen were scarce in the city at that time. Such a commotion now in that vicinity would fetch a dozen of them, as well as hundreds of citizens. As I could not persuade her to go and enter her complaint at the Station, I concluded to walk home with her, so taking the small bundle, we started on our long night's walk, with no electric lights as now.

She knew that I was her friend and told me how she came to be on that boat. Some of her neighbors told her if she wanted to get work in the city, all she had to do was to go to an intelligence office and they would get her a position. Her mother was a widow, and being poor, with nothing to do in the country, she thought, as she was fifteen years old, she could help her poor old mother keep their little home if she could get work. So that morning she had bid her tearful mother good-bye. She did not want her child to go, she would sooner starve. But the girl, like many others, was a little willful and thought she could take care of herself in the city, and that was the way she did it.

She went to the intelligence office, and they, caring nothing for the girl except to get their fee, persuaded her to go as cook on the captain's boat, for he had just then applied for one, and she went along with him, as innocent of harm as though she was with her own father or brother. After being aboard a short time she began to consider her position, and the rough talk of the captain had opened her eyes, and the sad looks when I came in for supper, was the consequence.

I know not what would have been the outcome if I not providentially arrived upon the scene as I did, and the poor girl was about tired out before arriving at her home, near morning, having travelled the same road twice that day, besides the experience and one dollar out for her fee at the intelligence office.

But she bravely plodded on, stopping to rest occasionally. She had ample time to acquaint me with her history. She had not obeyed her mother in going to the city. With tears in her eyes she said she would sooner starve than ever visit the city again without a protector.

I was not much of a philosopher in those days, but I told her that to obey her mother and listen to her counsels, would be the greatest protector she could ever get. We walked upon the towing path of the canal from the rapids until we came to what is now the River View House, then turned off on the river road and arrived at her home a mile or so up the river. She awakened her mother, and the "God blessings" I received after acquainting her of her daughter's escape from the drunken captain, if worth anything, would put a regiment of sinners through purgatory. I believe they were good for something however, as I felt like a hero after the praises that were heaped upon me by those poor people.

They rigged me a bed upstairs and although near morning, I had quite a rest before coming down to breakfast, which must have been near noon. The simple menu consisted of baked potatoes, gravy and tea, but the grateful looks of both mother and daughter sufficed for bread and dessert. No one with plenty of wealth and relations could have received more blessings and tears when going to the wars, than were given to me when parting from them that day. All the wealth I owned then was good health, a good trade of boatmanship, six dollars and a little change, but no home, and no berth on any boat, as I had sacrificed my position engaged the previous night, but I left them a five dollar bill.

They did not want to take it, and would not until I told them I had plenty in the bank. My bank was the banks of the canal and the money could only be drawn after I had steered a boat through them.

I walked back to the city, arriving there at about three or four P.M. I was weaving air castles all along the road, about how I would someday come back to see my little sweetheart, as I now thought of her. That was young man fashion, but it never materialized, for I never saw them again.

I looked for the boat on which I had hired out, but she was gone. The skipper must have routed out someone who had opened his prison doors, hired help, and gone to Pittsford to load. Then I conceived the brilliant plan, being out of a job, of going down and hiring out to him again, for it being dark when he hired me, he could not recognize me only by my voice, and being as drunk as he was, he probably could not have done it by that. If he had not hired a man yet, my chances would be good, as well as a good joke on the captain.

But I did not get to Pittsford, for at Brighton locks I hired out to John Packard, captain of a Western Transportation Co.'s boat, the "New Jersey", loaded with wheat for New York.

I did not know the name of the boat upon which I had the adventure with the drunken captain, nor did I know his name. I only knew it was a Rochester ball head boat, but could never know it if I met it, as there were so many of them built just alike.

A few years ago I delivered a lecture in a schoolhouse in that neighborhood, and went to the house I was pretty sure was the one my rescued girl and her mother had lived in. It looked like the place only improved, with additions built on it, and when giving the young lady a lecture bill, I asked her if she ever knew of a widow and her daughter living there.

"What were their names?" she asked.

I could not tell her. If I ever did know, I had forgotten.

She said she never knew of any residing there.

After getting some distance from the house I figured up the time passed since that ever-to-be-remembered night, and realized the passing of time. It must have been near fifty years, and I felt absurdity of asking that woman about the family that had lived there undoubtedly twenty-five years before she was born. The question must have been asked as in a dream.

The reader can see that the inland waters of navigation are not devoid of adventures. They have their lovers, their mysteries, and crimes, as well as any other section of the country. The above narrative would furnish material for a first-class novel. I have had many other adventures, but none as exciting in so short a time.

The Girl Who Caused a Fight

Excerpted from *Rochester and its Early Canal Days* by Capt. H.P. Marsh (1914).

This story, true in every detail, commences in the city of Buffalo, the western terminal of the Erie Canal. It was in the summer of 1862, when our country was in the throes of that terrible Civil War. Boating at that time was the best it had ever been. Freights were the highest and all water crafts were running at their greatest capacity. Boats at that time carried crews of six: a captain, two drivers, two steersmen, and a cook.

Two boats were loaded with wheat and were moving slowly along at sundown until coming to the canal grocery, where they stopped and the captains went ashore for supplies. The head boat was named The *Octoroon* out of New York, run by Captain Dan Somers. There was no woman for cook, but the other boat, named the *Oriole*, had a beautiful woman to serve in that capacity, the captain's wife, Mrs. Ada Loverage.

After supper, Captain Mark Loverage told his crew they had better turn in for a good night's rest, for they would start very early in the morning. Captain Dan came on deck, lighted a cigar, and said to the crew of the other boat, "Come on, boys, with us. Let's go down on Canal Street to a dance house for a little while."

He did not invite Captain Mark as he knew he would not go. They, being friends, always tried to keep their boats as nearly together as possible, although their characters were the opposite.

Mark Loverage was a gentleman, and his wife a lady, and they moved in the best society in the city of Rome, Oneida County, while Captain Dan was fond of his whiskey, and somewhat of a loafer or sporting man. "Come on, Hank Millions, let's have some fun," he says, beckoning to one of the steersmen aboard the *Oriole*.

"No," says Hank, "I have no use for Canal Street."

"All right," says Dan, "be a saint if you want to. Come on, boys." He jumped ashore, followed by his crew.

Ada, who was seated in the hatch, gently clapped her hands and said in a low voice, heard only by Hank, he being near the stern of the boat, "Oh, I'm so glad!"

Hank looked up, and seeing her, asked her why she was so pleased.

"Because I believe you are too much of a gentleman to disgrace yourself by going to such places."

All who knew Buffalo at that time were aware that nearly all the habitations on Canal Street were houses of ill-fame. "You and Jack are so much different," said she, "from all the other steersmen we ever had. You neither drink nor swear, and must have had better bringing up than most canal boatmen. You keep yourselves well dressed and stay with us longer. We can trust you in port or afloat."

"I appreciate your opinion," replied Hank, "and am glad we were not educated for loafers, and although I feel that your compliments are undeserved by me, I shall endeavor by God's help not to disgrace myself, or get lower in the scale of humanity than I now am." The captain coming aft just then, put a stop to the conversation.

Henry Millions, usually called Hank, and his partner, Jack Needham, the other steersman, were dispositioned very much alike: quiet, good-hearted, temperate young men, rather a scarce article those days on the canal. Their tastes were similar, rather be reading when not at work than laying around public places. Both were about the same size; rather under medium; and although not quarrelsome, each had the courage to stand up for their rights or for the rights of their captain. Never were they known to back down when in the right or to be second best in a fight if it came to that.

Although sociable, and apparently enjoying life, there was in each face a sadness of expression, as though some deep grief was ever present in their thoughts. Perhaps that was the reason for their being such good friends, being able to sympathize with each other, although they never confided their secrets, one to the other, if they had any.

The crew of the *Oriole* was up early the next morning and aroused the other boat's crew, but not easily, as they had been out nearly all night carousing. The boats were under way by daylight, and while waiting for the lock at Black Rock, the crew of the *Oriole* saw a woman on the *Octoroon*, apparently getting breakfast.

Knowing that Captain Dan had no wife, they concluded he had hired a cook while ashore the previous night. When changing horses at 7 A.M., they ran close alongside of Captain Dan's boat, and saw a young and pretty girl, officiating as mistress of the boat.

Ada said, "Oh! What a shame to have that young girl on board with those rowdies."

The rest of the crew coincided with her opinion. Jack said to his chum, when changing tricks at the tiller, "If Captain Dan's cook was old and tough-looking, it would be all right, but to think he has got such a nice-looking girl is beyond my comprehension."

"Perhaps it's his sister," said Hank.

"Well, whoever she is, she apparently wants to be there," concluded Jack.

At Middleport, where the boats stopped to buy oats and groceries, they lay side by side, so the cabins were close together. Then what did Mrs. Loverage do, but start a conversation with the new cook, who she learned was about sixteen years old, and a farmer's daughter, who lived in the town of Manchester, near Palmyra. She had been influenced by a girl somewhat older to leave her home and go to Buffalo. She did so under the pretense of visiting her married sister in Palmyra. After their money ran out they took the advice of a man, and fetched up on Canal Street. They were young and rather wild, but as bad as they were, Canal Street disgusted them and the Manchester girl thought she had better get away from there. She in some way came across Captain Dan, and hired out to cook on his boat.

Ada coaxed the girl to leave that degrading position at the first favorable opportunity, and go home. She promised to do so. The boats soon separated and kept apart until Rochester was reached. A crowd of boats was there, waiting their turn to be locked through.

The girl came aboard the *Oriole* to see Ada, who still advised her to leave the *Octoroon* and come aboard the *Oriole* until they arrived at Palmyra at her sister's. She also made her realize her depraved condition, and with tears streaming down her face, she promised to do as Ada told her, but went back to her boat to avoid suspicion.

Captain Dan seemed rather pleased to think Ada would notice his cook. His pleasure was soon over, for at the lower lock at Brighton, his cook with her little bundle of clothes, jumped ashore and ran back up the canal. When the captain saw her, he told his crew to stop the boat below the lock and wait for him. He then started on the run after her.

The *Oriole* was just coming out of the middle lock at Brighton. Ada, who was on deck and expecting the girl, told her husband to stop the boat and get her. The captain and his crew had heard from Ada the girl's story, and lost no time in obeying orders from his wife.

Both steersmen jumped ashore with pikepoles, while the captain and driver stopped the boat and ran a plank ashore. Captain Dan had just caught the screaming girl, when steersman Hank came up and made him loosen his grasp. The captain then made a lunge for Hank, who promptly knocked him down. Jack came up to help his partner steersman, who said, "Get the girl aboard, I will attend to the captain," who was knocked down every time he got up.

Captain Mark then came up and put a stop to the fight. Captain Dan slunk away to his own boat, pretty well used up, cursing the *Oriole's* crew, Hank in particular, swearing he would get revenge sometime. Thus ended the friendship of the two boats.

The girl was cheered up and made as comfortable as possible, until the boat arrived at Palmyra the next day. The *Oriole* tied up at the dock, near the collector's office, which was a little west of where now stands Cleavland's Canal Grocery. Ada went with the girl to her sister's, which was not far from the canal. The sister had not heard that the girl had left home until informed of it by Ada.

The wanderer asked her sister's forgiveness, and the sister in turn promised never to let the parents know but what she had been with her all of the time. It would have done no good, and made them feel very badly, to learn of their youngest daughter's escapade, and undoubtedly they were always kept in ignorance of it. She was gone only a week, but nevertheless had in all probability learned considerable in that brief time of human depravity.

She tearfully parted with her benefactor, who tripped lightly back to her floating home, where she was welcomed by the whole crew, who looked upon her as superior to most of the human race; and was she not? How few there are in church or out of it that would care, or do as did Ada Loverage. Many, even professing Christians, are too absorbed in their own affairs, or too dignified to throw out a helping hand.

Christ says, "I came to call sinners to repentance, not the righteous." Ada Loverage was one of His true followers, believed in helping the downcast and sinful, and in this case her efforts were crowned with success, for the writer lived some years in Palmyra and learned that this wayward girl married and lived happily with her husband, respected by all her neighbors, who undoubtedly never heard of her experience.

The Colored Man and His Bible

Excerpted from the missionary account in *Five Years on the Erie Canal: An Account of Some of the Most Striking Scenes and Incidents, During Five Years' Labor on the Erie Canal* by M. Eaton (1845).

I once gave a colored man a Bible, as I have been in the habit of giving all colored men whom I met on boats either a Bible or Testament. This man was a very profane one, and when I gave him the Bible, I told him I hoped it would be the means of breaking him of that sin. He seemed very thankful for the Bible, and said he had none; that he had a wife and children, and intended to carry it home to them.

Several months afterwards, I happened upon the same boat again, when a colored man reached out his hand to me and exclaimed, "Master, some d—d villain has stolen the Bible you gave me, and I wish he was in h—l!" He continued to curse and swear about it.

Said I to him, "Stop! Do you know what you are saying? You are as bad as the man who stole your Bible. I gave it to you for the purpose of doing you good, but I think you have not read it much, for if you had, instead of wishing the man who stole it in endless misery, you would wish it might be the salvation of his soul. Only think what a wish you have made! Had you not much rather he would reflect on the crime he has committed in stealing your good book, and while he reads it, see that he stole the denunciations of God against the thief? Would you not rather have the thought prove an arrow in his soul, and be the means of saving it from hell? Then he would return your Bible."

I then related to him a circumstance of a colored man who stole a very nice gilt Bible from a passenger while going up Lake Erie. The passenger had been reading in the Bible before he left it in the cabin, and while he was on deck the cook saw it, and the temptation was so great that he stole it. When the passenger inquired for his Bible, no one had seen it.

The gentleman very mildly remarked, "Never mind the Bible, the man who has taken it will have more trouble about it than I shall, for I intend to pray to God that he may not have one moment of peace or comfort until he repents, not only of the crime of stealing my Bible, but of all his sins. And," continued he, "I believe God will hear my prayer; and if the thief is only converted, my Bible is well disposed of." This was said in the presence of the man who had stolen the Bible and while they were looking for it, sure enough, it troubled almost insupportably, as he acknowledged afterwards.

After the gentleman had left the steamboat, the thief undertook to read the Bible which he had stolen, but every sentence condemned him not only for stealing, but for lying about it. His trouble increased, until he wished he had never seen that Bible, and he tried to find some hiding place, but the more he sought to hide himself, the more he was convinced that God saw him. At length he concluded that there was but one alternative, so he took the Bible, opened it, fell on his knees, and confessed to God that he was a poor, wretched sinner.

His distress continued until he became willing to cast himself upon the mercy of God, and then God had mercy on him. After his conversion, he wrote to the gentleman whose Bible he had stolen, confessing his guilt, and saying he would return it, and pay him whatever sum he would name. The gentleman wrote him in reply that he was welcome to keep the Bible or to give it away, as he pleased, for that he was well rewarded for the loss he had sustained.

The colored man to whom I was telling this story replied, "That was a good one, but I am afraid God would not hear my prayer, I am so wicked."

I told him not to borrow any trouble about one Bible, for that I would give him another one, the first time I should see him. He seemed well pleased with the idea of having another Bible, and said he, "I hope God will serve the man that stole my Bible, as he did that other darkey, and then I guess he bring him back."

"That is right," said I, "and you should pray for the man." About one year afterwards, I was on the same boat again, and the colored man seemed glad to see me. I asked him if he had found his Bible yet.

He said, "No, but God would convert the man who stole it. Oh, how wicked I was," said he, "to wish that man in hell. I thought about it a great many times, and have had great deal trouble about it. I kept trouble more and more, until I could not sleep, I have so much cry to make, to think of wish I made. I pray God forgive me. I hope he has. I can pray now, and not have any trouble. I don't wish no man any bad. All I wish, I hope all be converted, and then steal no more Bibles." He told me he had united with the church, and he seemed to be very much changed.

Thus we see the passage fulfilled, "The wrath of man shall praise Him." The simple story told by this colored man gave me much satisfaction, and from what I saw and learned of him from others, I have good reason to believe that his wish with regard to the man who stole his Bible, was the means of the salvation of his soul. He was so much troubled about it, that he was led to see his own sins, and to seek salvation in the blood of Christ.

"God brings men by the way they know not of." It is often the case, that men are converted by means of their own wickedness, as in the case above referred to, and if profane men would only reflect a moment, after they have been calling on God to damn their own souls, or the souls of others, it does seem that many more of them would be led to repentance.

My prayer is that when the sinner reads of these circumstances, and sees the mercy of God in the conversion of the man who stole the Bible, and of the one who wished the thief in hell for stealing his Bible, he may inquire of himself, "Am I a sinner, and will that God whom I have so often abused, grant me a pardon for my sins? If I seek, shall I find the pearl of great price?"

Let me ask, what is more noble for a man, when he has done a wrong, than to confess it? God is ever ready to forgive the sinner, when he comes to the feet of Jesus. If all men were as willing to confess as God is to forgive them, how many quarrels and disputes would be dispensed with! Where is the man who is so hardened that he would refuse to forgive his neighbor, when he came as an honest man and confessed his faults? If he should refuse to do it, he would be considered in the sight of God, worse than the man who had done the wrong.

Books by Donna Winters

For the Love of Roses

Mackinac

The Captain and the Widow

Sweethearts of Sleeping Bear Bay

Charlotte of South Manitou Island

Aurora of North Manitou Island

Bridget of Cat's Head Point

Rosalie of Grand Traverse Bay

Isabelle's Inning

Elizabeth of Saginaw Bay

Jenny of L'Anse Bay

Unlikely Duet

Butterfly Come Home

Fayette - A Time to Love

Fayette - A Time to Laugh

Fayette - A Time to Leave

Bluebird of Brockport, A Novel of the Erie Canal

Donna Winters invites readers to contact her through her website or blog:

http://www.GreatLakesRomances.com

greatlakesromances.blogspot.com

You can write to her at:

Donna Winters
PO Box 85
Garden, MI 49835

Made in the USA
Charleston, SC
08 July 2012